CCSS Genre Dram

Essential Que

What can you discover w..... ,
a second look?

MW01142148

The Surprise PARTY

by Feana Tu'akoi
illustrated by James Watson

Act 1
The Clues
Scene 1 2
Scene 2 5

Act 2
Following the Trail
Scene 1 8
Scene 2 11

Act 3
The Party
Scene 1 14

Respond to Reading. 16

PAIRED READ The Clothes Thief 17

Focus on Literary Elements 20

Act 1
The Clues

CHARACTERS

JACOB and **CALEB** (brothers)
VERA and **MIGUEL** (**JACOB** and **CALEB's** friends)
SECURITY GUARD
ENRIQUE (librarian)
MIKE (youth-group leader)
CELIA (**JACOB** and **CALEB's** mom)
GRANDMA J. (owner of the house, **JACOB** and
   CALEB's grandmother)

—————— Scene 1 ——————

Scene: **GRANDMA J.'s** living room
JACOB, CALEB, and **MIGUEL** are lounging around,
looking bored. They are wearing costumes. **VERA,** also
dressed in costume, enters and flops onto a chair.

VERA: (yawning) Any word on the party? Do we know
   where it's going to be yet?

JACOB: No, I've just checked. The e-mail hasn't arrived.

MIGUEL: (grumpy) How much longer is it going to take?
   We've been hanging around for ages.

VERA: (nodding) I thought we'd have heard something by
   now. Do you think the party has been called off?

JACOB: (shaking his head) I don't think so. Mike would
   have told us. He knows we're waiting for the e-mail.

CALEB: (frowning) I don't know why Mike didn't just
   fill us in last night. It would have made things
   much easier.

JACOB: Maybe he was finalizing things. There might still have been some details to figure out.

VERA: (*grinning*) No, I think he's doing it on purpose to keep us on edge. You know how Mike loves to be mysterious!

Sound effect of an e-mail arriving.

JACOB: (*jumping up*) Hold on! That's an incoming message sound. Yep, an e-mail just came through.

> **JACOB** *sits down at the computer.* **MIGUEL**, **VERA**, *and* **CALEB** *look over* **JACOB's** *shoulder.*

MIGUEL: So, what does it say?

JACOB: (*perplexed*) The e-mail says that we should leave right away. The party will be held nearby.

VERA: Nearby? That's not very precise. What kind of clue is that?

CALEB: It's no clue at all. How will we know where to go?

JACOB: Maybe we have to wander around the neighborhood until we see a sign or hear a party. Parties can be pretty loud.

MIGUEL: (*shaking his head*) That doesn't sound right. There must be more information. Jacob, see if you can scroll down any farther.

JACOB: (*moving the mouse and nodding*) Oh, here we go. First there's a smiley face. Then it says, "Please follow the clues."

CALEB: That sounds more like it. What's next?

JACOB: The clue is: "A place full of learning." Period. (*moving the mouse and checking the screen*) I've scrolled down to the bottom. There's nothing else.

VERA: (*grinning*) A place full of learning? Too easy! The party is going to be at our school.

CALEB: That's it!

Everyone nods in agreement. **MIGUEL** *high-fives* **VERA**.

MIGUEL: Great work, Vera! Let's go!

MIGUEL *exits, and the others follow close behind.*

Scene: *Outside the school*
CALEB, **JACOB**, **MIGUEL**, *and* **VERA** *stand outside the gates. The* **SECURITY GUARD** *waits offstage.*

JACOB: Hey, the school's all locked up.

CALEB: (*rolling his eyes*) Everyone is on vacation, Jacob. What did you expect?

JACOB: (*grinning at his brother*) I mean, how can the party be here if the school's closed?

VERA: I didn't think of that. Maybe one of the other gates is open.

MIGUEL: Come on, Vera. Let's go check it out.

MIGUEL *and* **VERA** *exit.*

CALEB: (*rubbing his chin*) Hmmm, that's weird.

JACOB: What's weird?

CALEB: I've been thinking about that e-mail, and I've thought of something strange.

JACOB: What do you mean?

CALEB: The instructions said to follow the clues, plural, but there was only one clue in the e-mail.

JACOB: Hey, you're right! There was definitely only one clue. I checked. So where are the other clues?

CALEB: Maybe the first clue wasn't meant to take us to the party after all. Maybe there is a whole series of clues that we have to find, one after the other.

JACOB: (*nodding*) The next clue could be hidden around here somewhere! Come on, let's look for it.

JACOB and CALEB look around for another clue. They check in all directions, looking under and behind things.

CALEB: (*spreading his hands out*) Well, I've got nothing. Maybe this wasn't such a great idea after all.

JACOB: (*sighing*) If a clue were here, we would have found it.

CALEB: Look, here come the others.

MIGUEL enters with VERA.

MIGUEL: We checked all the gates, and the whole place is locked up tight.

VERA: (*nodding*) There's no way a party is here today.

SECURITY GUARD: (*walking onstage*) Hey! What are you kids up to, all dressed up like that?

VERA: We're trying to find a party. The clue said that it was at a place full of learning, but the school is locked.

CALEB: (*nodding*) We thought there might be another clue hidden around here someplace, but we can't find anything.

SECURITY GUARD: (*thinking for a moment*) A place full of learning? It might not be the school, you know. It's not really full of learning during summer vacation. Maybe you should reconsider your clue and look at it from a different angle.

MIGUEL: (*surprised*) You might be right! Thanks for your help.

SECURITY GUARD: No problem! I hope you find your party. Good luck.

The **SECURITY GUARD** *smiles and exits.*

VERA: This is tough. Where else could the party be? The e-mail said it would be somewhere nearby.

JACOB: But how can a place be full of learning?

CALEB: If we just knew what kind of learning, then we could figure out what kind of place it is.

They all sit down to think.

MIGUEL: (*jumping up*) I've got it! Books are full of learning; aren't they? The clue might mean the library!

JACOB: (*unconvinced*) A party at the library? I'm not so sure. Libraries are quiet places. How would people concentrate with a party going on?

VERA: (*shrugging*) It's the best idea we have, and it makes sense with the clue. Let's go check it out.

The others nod and follow **VERA** *as she exits.*

Following the Trail

--------- Scene 1 ---------

Scene: *The library*

JACOB, **CALEB**, **VERA**, *and* **MIGUEL** *are standing in the doorway.* **ENRIQUE**, *the librarian, is working.*

VERA: Those people over there are staring.

CALEB: Well, we do look kind of strange!

JACOB: (*looking around the library*) There's no party here.

MIGUEL: Well, I'm all out of ideas.

CALEB: Let's ask Enrique.

> **ENRIQUE** *looks up and jumps back with surprise.*

ENRIQUE: Whoa, great costumes! I'm astounded by your creativity.

VERA: Thanks, Enrique. We need your help.

MIGUEL: (*nodding*) We were following a clue that's supposed to lead us to a party. We were convinced the party was at school, but no one was there.

ENRIQUE: As my mom always says, if at first you don't succeed, try, try again.

CALEB: Exactly. So we looked at the clue again and tried to interpret it differently.

VERA: But it looks as if we got it wrong *again*. The clue is: "A place full of learning." Any ideas?

ENRIQUE: Maybe you should be looking closer to home. (*holding out a printout of an e-mail*) Mike said you'd be dropping by. He asked me to give you this.

MIGUEL: Thanks, Enrique! (*looking at the printout*) It's another clue: "Children will laugh in the sunshine."

CALEB: (*groaning*) Oh, no! Here we go again. Will we ever make it to this party?

VERA: (*grinning*) Think positively! We solved the first clue, so we can solve this one. We just need to consider it from all angles.

JACOB: I know a place where kids are always laughing.

MIGUEL: Is it nearby?

JACOB: Sure is. In fact, it's right next door.

CALEB: The games arcade? You're right. That's a fun place, and watching you trying to win certainly makes me laugh.

JACOB: (*grinning*) Ha, ha. Come on, let's go!

VERA: Hold on. What happened to considering things from all angles? The games arcade is inside, so there's no sunshine.

MIGUEL: And it says that they *will* laugh—as if it will happen in the future, not now or in the past.

CALEB: Hmmm, I can think of a place where kids will have fun in the sunshine, but they can't yet because it's not finished.

JACOB: Of course! The new playground they're building on our street. Come on, everybody, follow me!

JACOB *leads the group offstage.*

Scene: *The playground site*

VERA, **JACOB**, **CALEB**, *and* **MIGUEL** *are looking uncomfortably hot in their costumes as they stand on the playground site.*

MIGUEL: (*pulling at his costume*) This playground sure is sunny. I'm starting to cook!

VERA: Me, too. Let's stand in the shade of that tree while we figure out what to do.

They all move into the shade.

MIGUEL: (*looking around the playground site*) No one is around to give us another clue. Are you sure we've come to the right place?

CALEB: (*nodding*) This has to be the right place. It makes perfect sense. It's a place in the sunshine where children will laugh. But there's no party here now, so there must be a hidden clue. All we have to do is find it.

MIGUEL: (*sighing*) Everyone, start searching!

They all start searching for the clue.

VERA: (*wiping her brow*) I can't find anything, and I'm so hot. I'm going to have to rest under the tree.

VERA lies down under the tree and stares up through the branches.

CALEB: Don't give up now, Vera. It's got to be around here somewhere.

VERA: (*laughing*) Who said I was giving up? I was looking for the clue, and guess what? I've found it!

VERA stands up and points upward. A paper is taped to one of the branches.

JACOB: (*climbing up and taking the paper*) Great work, Vera!

CALEB: What does it say? I hope it tells us where to go for the party because I'm starving!

JACOB: (*unfolding the paper*) It says, "Last clue! A house of history."

VERA: That's easy! It's the museum.

CALEB: I don't think so, Vera. It has to be somewhere nearby. The museum is too far away for us to reach on foot.

VERA: You're right. I didn't think of that. Where else could it be?

MIGUEL: I can't think of any place like that around here.

VERA: This is just like the library clue. We need to look at it in another way.

JACOB: Maybe it's not a building with historic things in it. Maybe it's just an ordinary house that's been around for ages.

MIGUEL: Or a house that was involved in history somehow—kind of like a monument. You know, a place where something really important happened.

JACOB: (*staring at* **MIGUEL**) Miguel, you're a genius! I know exactly where the party is! Think about it! There's a house we all know that's historically important. It's a house with a secret room where enslaved African Americans were concealed when they escaped to the North.

CALEB: (*grinning*) Oh, I get it now!

JACOB: (*nodding*) That's right—it's Grandma J.'s house! I think we have a party to go to!

> **JACOB** high-fives **CALEB** and exits.
> Everybody else follows.

Act 3
The Party

Scene: GRANDMA J.'s *living room*

MIGUEL, **VERA**, **CALEB**, *and* **JACOB** *arrive at the house. The furniture is pushed back to the sides of the room, the walls are decorated, and music is playing.*
MIKE, **GRANDMA J.**, *and* **CELIA** *wait offstage.*

MIKE: (*jumps onstage*) Surprise!

JACOB: Ahhh! Wow, this is a surprise all right. This is the last place we expected to have the party.

VERA: We're back where we started. Who knew?

MIGUEL: Look at the place. You've moved the furniture, decorated the room, and—best of all—there's all this great food.

CALEB: I can't believe you've done so much so quickly. How did you organize all this without making us suspicious?

MIKE: I had a lot of help.
(*gesturing to people offstage*)
Come over here, you two. Tell them how you helped.

CELIA *and* **GRANDMA J.** *enter, grinning.*

CELIA: (*shrugging*) I didn't do much. Mike came up with the idea, went shopping, and moved all the furniture.
I just put up a few decorations and laid out the food.

MIKE: Don't be so modest. I couldn't have done it without you. You did tons of work.

MIGUEL: (*looking around the room*) This place looks amazing.

VERA: There's enough food to feed our whole school!

JACOB: (*nodding*) You're telling me. What about you, Grandma J.? What did you do?

GRANDMA J.: I didn't do much, either. I just made up a few clues and e-mailed them to Mike. I thought inquisitive children like you would get a kick out of solving a puzzle.

MIKE: (*grinning*) She sent me a different set of clues for each group. The clues spread you out all over town. She didn't want you to run into each other in case you figured it out too quickly. All I did was forward them to everyone.

CALEB: (*groaning*) No wonder we had so much trouble with the clues. When it comes to puzzles, Grandma J. is the best!

VERA: (*nodding*) Those clues really got us thinking. We had to keep looking at them in different ways to solve them.

CELIA: I can hear some of the others arriving.

GRANDMA J.: It sounds as if they had fun, too.

VERA: (*grinning*) We all had such a good time getting here that it's bound to be a great party!

MIKE: Let's surprise them. Come on, everybody, hide!

Everybody follows **MIKE** *as he exits.*

Respond to Reading

Summarize

Use important details from *The Surprise Party* to summarize how the characters figured out the clues they found. Your graphic organizer may help you.

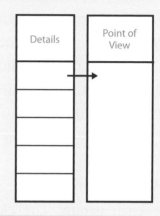

Text Evidence

1. What features show you the text is a drama? GENRE

2. By the end of Act 1, Scene 2, what points of view do Caleb, Jacob, Vera, and Miguel have? Explain what each character says that expresses his or her point of view. POINT OF VIEW

3. What does "if at first you don't succeed, try, try again" on page 8 mean? What clues in the dialogue help you figure it out? ADAGES

4. In the final scene, Mike, Grandma J., and Celia discuss how they prepared for the party. Write to compare Mike's point of view about the work the women did with their own points of view about that. WRITE ABOUT READING

Compare Texts

Read about a mystery in which someone needs to take a second look.

The Clothes Thief

"Hey, Nan," Tyler yelled, "did you take my blue T-shirt? I left it on the chair in my bedroom and now it has disappeared."

"First your sweater, then your jacket, and now your T-shirt," Nan said, looking perplexed. "I wish you'd take better care of your clothes."

"But I know I didn't lose them," Tyler complained. "Somebody must have stolen them."

Nan sighed and shook her head with disbelief.

"No burglar would break in and steal your old clothes," she said. "And, Tyler, please be careful with Ralph. We agreed when you adopted him that he'd live outside, but there is hair all over this bedroom."

Nan placed a laundry basket on the chair.

"Oh, and Tyler," she added, "Please hang these jeans on the clothesline before you go. You'll certainly need them for school tomorrow."

Tyler stomped his way downstairs and scowled as he hung up his jeans. It wasn't fair—he didn't lose his clothes, and he didn't let Ralph into his room in spite of wanting to.

Illustration: Lorenzo Van Der Lingen

The new school year had gotten off to a difficult start for Tyler. He'd picked up Ralph from the animal shelter only a few weeks earlier, so it was tough having to leave him on his own so soon. To make matters worse, Tyler was now being blamed for things he had not done.

When Tyler returned home that afternoon, Nan reported that she was worried about Ralph. "He hardly came out of that dirty house bed all day," she said. "Though I must say he seems to have recovered now."

Tyler collected a tennis ball and rushed outside to play with his dog. He'd only thrown the ball a couple of times when he saw several clothespins on the ground and noticed that his jeans were now missing.

"Hey, Nan," he called, "did you take my jeans inside?"

Nan looked out the window and shook her head. Tyler couldn't believe it, Now his clothes were being stolen from the clothesline! He decided to set a trap. He went inside, got his favorite shirt, and hung it on the line.

"Come on, Ralph," he said. "Let's do some detective work so we can show the thief that crime doesn't pay." Tyler and Ralph concealed themselves in the shed for more than an hour, but no one suspicious entered the yard. His favorite shirt stayed exactly where he had left it.

"Maybe the thief realizes it's a trap," Tyler muttered.

"Aha," Nan announced, coming into the shed. "I wondered where you'd disappeared to. Please clean Ralph's dog house this afternoon. He's even messier than you, if that's possible."

Tyler agreed without complaint because it was important to him to take good care of Ralph. Besides, the task would allow him to continue his surveillance of the clothesline and hopefully catch the elusive thief.

He collected the necessary cleaning supplies and lifted the dog house roof, but then he stopped and shouted with astonishment. There, stuffed into a corner of the dog house, were all of his missing clothes: his sweater, his jacket, his T-shirt, and his jeans—and they were all covered in dog hair.

Nan watched him extract them from the dog house one by one. "Ralph must have taken them because they smell like you," she said with a chuckle. "Ralph obviously wanted something to remind him of you while you were at school. Now we know what was wrong with him. He missed you!"

Tyler grinned and gave Ralph an enormous hug. "I missed you too, you great big hairy clothes thief!" he said.

Make Connections

How did Nan's suggestion help Tyler solve the problem of the missing clothes? ESSENTIAL QUESTION

Why did the children in *The Surprise Party* and Tyler in *The Clothes Thief* have to look at a problem in a different way in order to find what they were looking for? ESSENTIAL QUESTION

Focus on Literary Elements

Foreshadowing Writers of stories or dramas with a mystery in them often build suspense by giving their readers hints or clues about what is to come later in the story. This is called foreshadowing. Like a shadow that can be seen on the ground in front of you when the sun is behind you, the clues in a story can be seen before the real outcome is revealed.

Read and Find Reread page 8 of *The Surprise Party*. How does the author foreshadow the ending (that the party is to be held at Grandma J.'s house)?

Your Turn

Write another scene for the play *The Surprise Party* that includes additional foreshadowing about what is to come at the end of the play.